Directly Speaking About Bookings

The Ultimate Booking Bible for Direct Sellers

My Purpose

*I believe knowledge is power
and it is my job to share my knowledge,
in order to help empower others.*

Lisa Toovey

Party Plan PhD. ™

Table of Contents

Dedication   5

Introduction – The Art of Booking   9
   What is a Booking?   12

Part 1 – Getting Started   13
   I'm Not Playing Games with You   15
   Where Do I Start?   18
   The Action Calendar   20
   Levels of Influence   25
   Be A Booking Magnet   27
   Believe   29
   Paint a Picture   31
   Ten Up!   32
   Build Momentum   33
   Make Five Calls a Day   35
   Walk Into Your Next Season   36
   First Come, First Served!   37
   Be Your Own Hostess   39
   Postcards   41
   Keep It Fresh!   42
   Bookings Before Sales!   43
   Overbook   44

Part 2 – Asking for the Booking   45

I Would Love to get Your Opinion   47
Can You Help Me?   49
The "Tentative" Booking   50
Either/Or   52
If You Were to Have a Party?   53
Do You Have Your Calendar Handy   54
Is There Any Reason Why…?   55

Part 3 – Booking at Your Parties   57

Build Desire   59
Client File Card/Draw Slip   63
Booking Envelopes   67
Available Party List   68
Book and Hold Gifts   70
Stack the Hostess Benefits   72
Rebook Your Hostess   73
Objections   74
The Perfect Uniform   76

Part 4 – Post Party   77

Rate Your Hostess   79
Let Go   81
Customer Care Calls   83
Customer Rescue   87
10 Reasons You Don't Get Bookings   89

About the Author   91

Dedication

I dedicate this book to three very special and influential women in my life. They say that when the student is ready the teacher appears. Ironically for me all three women were named Anne. Looking back over my career, the universe has sent me some valuable teachings and "Anne" has delivered them.

The first teacher became my mentor. It is true that attending your first conference can change your life. That is where I met my first great teacher named Anne. I was a starry eyed country girl that had never been to a big city like Toronto. This certainly was a case of opposites attracting. She was polished, professional and successful. I was a little country girl who ran bare foot around the farm wearing daisy dukes and collecting eggs from the hen house.

Anne's "how to" class was just what I needed. She was beautiful, wearing a large elegant black hat, the kind I had only seen royalty wear. Well I guess she was Weekenders royalty, so her choice of accessories was perfect. I wanted to be just like her. One day my phone rang and it was Anne on the other end. I was speechless. Her call was in response to my thank you note. In a true act of gratitude and giving back, Anne chose to mentor me. I would unexpectedly receive her diarized call every month with perfect timing. She coached me to heights of success that I hadn't even yet envisioned. Anne helped me to grow a highly recognized multi-million dollar team. Over the next 15 years we became friends, travelled together, shared good times and bad. I still hear her words… "Is what you are doing right at this moment bringing you one step closer to your goal?"

The second teacher became my best friend. Anne and I met in the lineup back stage as we were waiting to receive our annual sales recognition. Like two giggly school girls we bonded over our common achievement. During this time frame our company only awarded the "Top 10 in Sales" with a trip. I finished number 3 in Canada and she squeaked in at number 10. We celebrated with our spouses on the most amazing winter holiday in Deerhurst, Ontario. Our friendship was a cross country one but the phone kept us connected. Anne taught me how to be passionate. We shared our goals, dreams and hopes. It was Anne's dream to become a Sales Manager. She worked very hard to join me on the leadership path. When she achieved her goal, we celebrated at the next Managers conference; we both had "arrived". That was the last time I saw her. God took her home, at the young age of thirty one, sending me into a grieving spiral for the next year. It is difficult for me articulate all she taught me. If I could only share one thing with you, it would be, to live your dreams. I keep a picture of Anne on my desk to remind me of that every day.

The third teacher has guided me to you. She is the woman who helped me cross the bridge from the field as a million dollar leader to the corporate side as a trainer. My decision to move my career in this direction stems from my personal motto "Knowledge is Power." You see, I feel it is my responsibility to share my knowledge to help empower others to success, just as the first Anne in my life empowered me. This part of my journey, would once again provide many lessons but, what it gave me most, was the confidence to share with you. For that I am forever grateful.

I am also grateful for the love, support and encouragement my husband and children have given me. You are my "WHY" and it is because of you that I have stretched beyond my wildest dreams. And a new journey begins...

Introduction
The Art Of Booking

In our fast paced social media driven society, I am fearful as a direct seller that the art of the booking parties, is being lost. It has been said over and over by many experts that bookings are the life line of your business. I believe that in the direct sales industry, this has not changed. What has changed is the technology that is now available to us to promote and advertise our business. Today communication moves faster, and is easier than ever before. So if it has gotten so easy to communicate with our customers why are we struggling to get bookings? I believe direct sellers are hiding behind their computer which is now the new phone phobia.

Have we forgotten that group appointments are how we book, sell and recruit? Now I am not a social media expert, and at risk of you judging me as old fashioned, but hear me out because I am a booking expert. I have held over 1800 group parties in my career. That is 1800 hosts who I have treated to a free shopping spree. With an average of ten guests in attendance that adds up to over 18,000 happy shoppers! Hopefully you haven't tossed this little booking bible aside and I've got your attention again. Let's just say I've had lots of practice. After 30 years in the industry, I feel like I have earned, a Party Plan PhD. In my opinion, social media should be viewed as one of the new exciting streams, in our multiple streams of income. Upon examining your company's compensation plan and training manual, you will discover tried and true ways to make money. Here are some of the most common:

1. Sell direct to a customer.
2. Sell at parties or open houses.
3. Sell at a trade show, business or country fair.
4. Outside orders (orders that arrived by phone, email or text).
5. Recruit, train and build your own team.
6. *NEW*...Social Media.

Add social media to your business practice but don't make it your **ONLY** practice. Designing a business website, writing a blog, creating a fan page, updating your Facebook status and Twitter messages are all fun and affordable ways to communicate. They can even help you to sell your product and recruit new customers and team members.

Now with all of that said I encourage you to take what you learn from this book and apply it to the social media side of your business. Every tip, technique and idea can be used at your parties and on your Facebook fan page or as a Twitter message. I give you ownership and my blessing to put your creative spin on my words! After all, as I always say; "A great idea only gets better when it is shared with someone else."

What is a booking?

No matter what you call it, a booking is a group appointment. Some companies use terms like presentation, dating, demonstration, show, trunk show, fashion show, girls night in, workshop, class, party, launch party, announcement party, catalogue party, online party etc... No matter what you call it a booking is an appointment to sell to a group of people.

If you think about it a booking is the ultimate form of networking. You have a friend (hostess), who endorses you and your company by inviting a group of her friends over, to share your product/service with. In essence, she is giving you six to ten referrals all at once. How beautiful is that? From this group you will book future parties, sell to new and existing customers and find new recruits to join your team. Creating booking momentum truly is the key to success. Without it, a direct seller will struggle, become frustrated and quit. It is my goal to teach you how to book new group appointments better known as parties and fill up your calendar.

PART 1

GETTING STARTED

I'm Not Playing Games with You

Okay, I have to be honest with you. I'm not a fan of booking games and nine out of ten times my customers weren't fans either. Please don't be offended. Let me explain where my aversion comes from: My mom loved to host parties for our neighbor who sold a fabulous line of kitchen products. We would get together, burp bowls, see new products, eat finger sandwiches and drink tea. I loved these parties, they were girly and fun. Dorothy may have been my very first mentor with the exception of one thing: She would start her parties by forming the guests into two competitive lines, then hand both team captains a pair of panty hose, and excitedly direct "on your mark, get set, go!" The winning team to get the panty hose on and off each member first would win a prize. This image is still burned into my memory. I might have only been ten years old at the time but I couldn't understand why she was doing this. I realize now she was playing an ice breaker designed to relax the group and not a game designed to book new parties but none the less, I've been scarred for life. When I joined my first company at the age of sixteen I decided that Dorothy's methods weren't for me. Zig Ziglar and Joyce M Ross quickly became one of my favorite authors as I studied the art of closing the sale.

Now don't get me wrong, booking games work great for some direct sellers. If it ain't broke don't fix it.

If you have a game that is working for you, I encourage you to use it to your benefit. They never worked as successfully for me as the tried and true basic booking scripts and techniques. I think it has a lot to do with the energy you give off. I felt uncomfortable doing them, so my customers felt uncomfortable playing them with me. I guess I felt more like a con-artist than my authentic self and it showed.

I built my first business in approximately 27 small towns with 15,000 residents or less. In some cases I would visit the town or village once or twice every couple of months. In other cases, may be only once per new product launch or new catalogue. When I played a booking game with a group, it was really difficult to play the same game again, because they were wise to my methods. So what does one do when the game stops working? Keep looking for new booking games or learn new skills that will increase your booking odds at every party.

Let me share with you has worked for me. When my calendar is full, I like it to be stable and I found that most of the bookings I obtained from a booking game, cancelled; outright cancelled, **NOT** postponed to another date. This is especially frustrating when working toward a sales goal, special incentive, earning a trip or having a monthly income goal. I discovered that I could reduce the shuffling and eliminate cancellations, by working with hosts who **REALLY** want to earn free product. After all, the cream always rises to the top! This is what booking techniques will do for your business. I'm a believer of quality over quantity. I would prefer to book six solid parties with six excited and committed hosts rather than book with twelve who feel like their arm got twisted and have them outright cancel. Datebook shuffling is a direct seller's rollercoaster nightmare. Keeping happy loyal customers, who keep coming back, ensures success. The women who cancelled lost their trust in me and rarely did business of any kind with me in the future.

"Where do I Start?"

There might be hundreds of fabulous booking techniques and scripts out there. In actuality, any technique used to make a sale can be used to secure a booking. The only difference is you are selling them on being a hostess instead of selling them on buying the product. One could say that if you are a good sales person, you will also be a good booker. Generally speaking, they go hand in hand. Examine the success of the top sellers in your company. They didn't get there because they only focused on making the sale. They are equally focused on filling their calendar with future group appointments that will bring the next sale to them.

To follow are the tried and true booking tips, scripts, and techniques that I've built my businesses with. A few of them I can take credit for creating but most of them have been handed down to me. In some cases I can give credit to the original author but in most I cannot. In the fashion industry it is common to hear 'everything that is old is new again'. I guess we could say the same about booking techniques too. Networking and sharing of ideas is not uncommon, it is in some cases openly encouraged by Direct Sales companies. There really isn't any copyright on any of the material out there, as we collectively own and enjoy it. Ironically some of the ideas that I have used successfully and even became my trademark were unsuccessfully used by the person who shared it with me. I guess what I am trying to say it that there is a wealth of information out there, the internet makes it easier than ever to access, so enjoy it. Remember my motto..."Knowledge is Power!" Now it is time to empower you.

The Action Calendar

It all begins with putting some action into your calendar. This is a practice that I did with every consultant in my downline, as it was part of my new consultant training, and part of our regular monthly meetings.

Before you can begin booking parties you need to know when you are available and what your goals are. Even the most casual business owner can benefit from setting a monthly booking and income goal. This is what keeps us moving forward. The minute we stop, our business stops. It is easy to toss in the towel when we have an empty calendar. I recall a team leader in my down line who simply got tired. Her business was very successful but raising 3 children, working a full time job, with a loving but unsupportive spouse, it was just too much. Her business and life were out of balance. She struggled as her party schedule took over. With the kids missing mom and a negative husband, instead of taking action she shut down, and stopped booking parties. It only took a few weeks before her calendar was empty. When I asked her how she felt about it, she responded with "well, no one is beating my door down to book parties!" That was her last season.

The Action Calendar helps a direct seller to take control, book only as many parties as you want/need and only on days you are available. This is an exercise in availability. To do it correctly you will need a month at a glance calendar, a green highlighter marker and a 3 x 5 index card.

Electronic calendars and smart phones are a great way to keep you organized but are ineffective as a booking tool. Investing in a month at a glance datebook from an office supply store is money well spent. It is impossible for your prospective hostess to visualize her family calendar on your smart phone or even her own. Put a month at a glance calendar in front of her and she will quickly calculate when her yoga class is, the kids swim lessons, soccer games and even her next pay day! With this visual in mind, she will cross reference against your available dates, find an available match and like magic she's booked.

Step 1

Using a pen, mark all important family commitments, appointments and holidays on the calendar. This ensures you don't accidently book a party on a date when you should be attending a special event. Think of the positive message this also gives. By diarizing these activities on the month at a glance, without speaking a word, you are telling everyone what your priorities are and that you run a successful but balanced business. We like to work with busy people and this calendar gives everyone the impression you are busy, no matter if you want to do 3 parties a month or 3 a week.

Step 2

Using a pencil, mark all of the existing business activities onto the calendar. This should include all training workshops, product launch events, open houses, fundraisers, monthly team meeting, conference calls and of course, all party bookings etc... For the party bookings list the hostesses first and last name and phone number as a quick reference.

Step 3

Using the green highlighter marker, colour in every date you are free to do a party. Now this is usually where I get a bit of resistance. You might be thinking, but I only want to do four parties a month and with six dates taken up with personal commitments that leaves me 20-21 days out of a month for bookings. That is correct! Remember this is only an exercise in availability. I'm not telling you to book 20 parties a month but, rather, for you to see when you can work your business.

The first time I did this exercise I was an Executive Sales Manager with a large team to take care of and suffering from a severe case of manager-itis. This is a fictional disease when a manager stops doing what got them to their current level of success (selling, booking and recruiting) and focuses too much time on the administrative side of being a leader. I was too busy being a Manager to hold more than a couple parties a month! A big old case of **REALITY** slapped me on the side the head when I did my first action calendar. I realized I wasn't leading by example and could easily add more parties into my schedule.

Step 4

On the index card down, the left hand side, write the days of the week Sunday through Saturday. Now transfer the dates from your month at a glance to the index card. This will give you at a glance all of the Mondays you are available etc... This cheat sheet can now be carried with you in your purse, gym bag or pocket, everywhere you go, ensuring you are always ready to book your next party.

Step 5

On the back of the index card write out your goals for the month. Include how many parties you want to hold, how much you want to sell, how much income you want to earn, how many new recruits you want to add to your team and any company incentives you want to earn. Also take a moment to consider what you will do with the money you earn. Is your goal to pay off your credit card, decorate your living room, make your car payment or save for vacation? This is your WHY and it is our most important goal of all as it drives us.

Step 6

Repeat. For 20 years I practiced this easy exercise at the beginning of each month working 3 months out. This kept me focused, goal oriented and achievement driven.

The Action Calendar helps you to discover your availability while setting your monthly goals and provides a month at a glance booking calendar for parties and a booking cheat sheet.

Levels of Influence

There are three levels of influence to building a successful business. Understanding all three levels and what naturally occurs in each step is vital to building a strong business. One of the first activities we do as a new business owner is create a F.R.A.N.K. list. A list of Friends, Relatives, Acquaintances, Neighbors, and Kids connections. This list of potential hosts and customers is known as your first level of influence.

People you know (1st Level), introduce you to people they know (2nd Level), they in turn introduce you to people you don't know (3rd Level). We all begin in 1st Level which is made up of friends, family, & acquaintances. It is <u>suicide</u> to stay in 1st Level! Success is determined by getting to 3rd Level as quickly as possible.

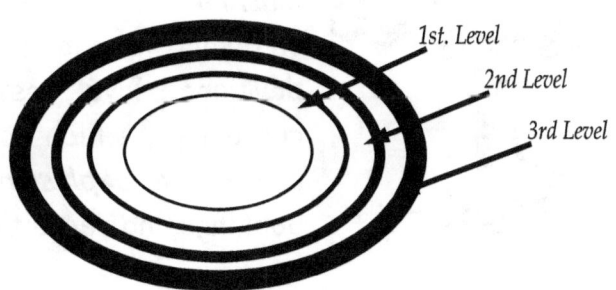

1st. Level

2nd Level

3rd Level

Unlike the first level of influence where you will book anyone and everyone to expand your network quickly, second level is more about fine tuning. There will be a natural culling of hosts and group. The people in your network who are not really interested in your product or being a host will fade away. This is a wonderful sign and natural evolution which is often misinterpreted as failure. While visiting the second level it is important to put your attention on hostess coaching and building a preferred client base that reflects your target market. This is where your *Ideal Hostess* list becomes your life line to the future. All too often, the second level is the stage that a direct seller will become frustrated and quit. Keep going because you've almost reached the pot of gold.

You will know when you have reached the third level

 when your business looks like a *mushroom*. It has been built on a solid foundation which has developed loyal hostesses and customers, which in turn has caused an *explosion* of sales, bookings and recruiting!

Be a Booking Magnet

Developing a booking mindset is crucial to filling your datebook. It is an attitude. It begins with your passion for the product and love of the company you represent. It is bigger than enthusiasm although enthusiasm is vital to success. If I could sum it up in one word that word would be **CONFIDENCE**. Practice makes perfect is true, but it also develops confidence, confidence in yourself, your product and your company's hostess program.

I believe visualization and self affirmation are critical to developing a booking mindset. You need to literally see yourself as a magnet. Got the visual? Now imagine in your mind's eye that you are a magnet that is walking down the street, everywhere you go people are becoming stuck to you. In the grocery line up, BAM, the checkout gal is stuck to your shoulder. At the doctor's office, BAM, the receptionist gets stuck to your left arm! Sitting on the sidelines of your daughter's soccer game, BAM, one of the moms gets stuck to your leg. Your next party, BAM, two guest jump off the couch and get stuck to you. The humor in this paints a great picture of you collecting hosts everywhere you go. So walk tall, exude your booking confidence, to create what you want.

"I am a booking magnet!"

"Bookings are everywhere!"

"With grace and ease, bookings are attracted to me!"

Believe

Armed with a new magnetic attitude and action calendar in hand, it is time to become a master creator, by attracting what you want. Belief is defined as acceptance by the mind that something is true or real, often underpinned by an emotional sense of certainty. Writing out your booking goal at the beginning of the month, sets forth your intentions to the universe, putting the wheels of creativity in motion. The most important factor here is that you must believe you can achieve (attract) what you have written.

Setting a booking goal was a hot topic during coaching sessions with the members of my downline. It was routine practice for us to discuss if they were on track to achieve their goals. One session in particular comes to mind. Natalie was a dynamic new recruit with very clear income goals. During one of our chats, she shared her struggles with filling her calendar and asked for my advice. By discussing her challenges and creating solutions, she was rejuvenated to hold a phone blitz. When I prompted, "So how many parties do you want to book in the next week?" She enthusiastically responded with, "Twenty!" Concerned she was giving me her wish and not a number she believed in, I asked, "Do you believe that?" She responded with a defeated "No". There is no way Natalie would have been successful in her phone blitz if she didn't have the belief system that she could do it.   Her goal was revised to a number she believed to be achievable.   One week later she proudly told me that she successfully booked ten new parties.   Her soaring confidence, new found motivation, and belief system all helped her to do it again the following week. In the end she booked twenty parties, just ten at a time.

One of the best ways to show your belief is to create a hostess package for each new booking you intend to obtain. My belief system was to always have ten or more future parties booked.   I always carried ten hostess planning packages in my briefcase. Like magic before I knew it I was out of packages and needing to create ten more!

"What you think about, you bring about!"

Paint a Picture

Painting a picture of your ideal hostess is a fun way to gain clarity while attracting what you want. One of my favorite exercises is to outline all of the qualities of the perfect host. Take a 5 x 8 inch index card. At the top of it write...

"I am in the process of attracting my ideal hosts:

Now start listing their positive qualities. Don't over think this exercise. As a matter of fact, the more you go with the flow, the better. List only the things you want.

My list included:

"Excited, fun, motivated, love the product, influencing, social, personable, enthusiastic, organized, positive attitude, loyal, organized, reminds her guests, always has 8 - 10 in attendance, $1000 party average, quickly returns my calls, checks in with me to finalize details, rebooks each season!"

Keep this list on your desk. Read it often while working in your office, before making booking calls, or hostess coaching calls. It is especially important to read if you get a postponement or cancellation because it is reminder of the type of host you are attracting. Sometimes a postponement or cancellation is just making room for your ideal host to book.

Ten Up!

One of the secrets to my success has always been to focus on having ten future bookings lined up. This is where the phrase "ten up" was coined from. I guarantee you will never run out of bookings if you are focused on being ten ahead. That is ten future parties, you set the time frame. If you are a casual business owner, this might mean ten parties in the next quarter. Working part time, a direct seller would goal to have ten lined up for the next six or eight weeks while full time direct sellers will focus on the next four weeks. What will ten future parties do for your business? Based on a $500 party average, ten future parties is $5000 in sales, that's $1250 in profit if you earn 25% commission. Ten future parties can produce eighty to one hundred shoppers **AND** ten, twenty, even thirty, new party bookings. Imagine the momentum this would give your business. Ten future parties would also generate twenty new recruit leads and, if followed up with correctly, will result in two or more new recruits. Ten parties lined up guarantees a strong, vibrant, thriving, profitable and successful business!

Build Momentum

The billion dollar question is: how do we create booking momentum? Well, what has always worked for me is to stack my parties up, holding as many as I can in a two week period. Normally I would goal to hold 2 parties a week but when my calendar was lean I would stack eight or ten into the first two weeks of the month. My next goal would be to book as many parties as possible so that I could fill up the last two weeks of the month. To build momentum some of those bookings will spill into the beginning of the next month.

When I joined Weekenders, I achieved my quick start challenge of holding five parties in my first two weeks of business. As a young mom with a new-born baby, I decided to focus on booking for the start of the next catalogue, when the baby would be old enough to leave with a babysitter. When I started my second season those five parties had produced thirty-five more bookings to be done in three months. Still stacking parties close together, I started my third season with seventy-five confirmed hosts. By the next fall, I had more bookings then possible days with 110 parties to be held. You guessed it; that was when I started to focus on recruiting a team.

The truth is you can never get too comfortable as a direct seller, no matter how long you have been with a company. In the sixteen years I was with Weekenders, I re-started my booking line up at least five times. That's right! Once every couple of years I would go back to basics and do the company quick start all over again. This kept my personal business healthy. It also gave me confidence in the company and my own training because the quick start program worked every time.

One of the things I love the most about having a direct sales business is that we get a "do-over" whenever we want one. All we have to do is decide to start again. At the beginning of a New Year, new season, new catalogue, heck, you can even start over at the beginning of the month. I challenge you to hold a Grand Re-Opening of your business with each new catalogue, just to celebrate being part of this incredible industry.

"If you don`t have enough bookings, you haven't asked enough people."

Make Five Calls a Day

If you don't have enough bookings, you just have not asked enough people. The best way to remedy this is to get on the phone. Early in my career I made it a practice to make five calls per day with the intention of finding new bookings. The inspiration for my five calls a day program came from a workshop I had attended. The speaker professed "If you want to double, even triple your business just make five business development calls per day!" I started my calling immediately and four weeks later went from being a casual business owner doing two shows per month to BIG TIME five to seven shows per week! I grew my business seventy-three percent and was the first consultant in my region to sell in excess of $100K from my home.

Walk Into Your Next Season

I quickly learned the value of always keeping a healthy calendar. One of the ways I did this was to hand select ten of my best hosts to help me launch every new catalogue. It feels amazing to 'walk' into your season locked and loaded and ready to grow.

There was one season that I didn't do this. I don't remember why I didn't have my calendar locked and loaded. What an eye opener that was for me! After years of walking easily and effortlessly into my season, I found myself struggling to get my parties lined up. I was losing time and money playing telephone tag and the datebook shuffle. Instead of focusing my phone time on confirming and coaching my hosts, I was looking for hosts to have parties. That was when I made a promise to myself to never let that happen again. I was stressed and frustrated hunting for parties. It was a horrible experience compared to what I was used to. Having those first ten parties ready to go allows your enthusiasm and passion to take centre stage, setting the tone for your entire season.

First Come, First Served!

Blocking your calendar is an ongoing technique that ensures that your open dates are filled in chronological order. Mastering this technique is very important to maintaining a full calendar. Make it a habit to only offer the next two available dates, in the next three to four week time frame. If those dates don't work, then offer the next, until you come to an agreement. Most companies help with this method by encouraging hosts to hold their parties in the next 30 days. Remember a booking isn't a booking unless you have a date. Never let them get away, even if you have to break this rule, and book them outside that time frame. Blocking is vital to maintain booking momentum once you have built it up.

Terry was a terrific gal on my team. She was a real team player who never missed a meeting. During the action calendar group exercise, I noticed she didn't have any hostess names written on her calendar. When I asked her about it, she shared with the group that she had lots of parties. Yup her sister was booking, a friend promised to have a party, and gal from work was going to host for her. She even had a stack of leads on her desk to follow up with from her last trade show. The truth is Terry didn't have any parties booked because she didn't have any dates written on the calendar. I suggested she follow up with her leads list and offer them a choice of two dates in the next three weeks, just to see what might happen. Four weeks later, at our next meeting, Terry proudly reported that she had three hosts penciled into her calendar.

"Remember a booking isn't a booking unless you have a date penciled into your calendar."

Be Your Own Hostess

Now this may not be a new idea, but it is tried and true. Every direct sales company will tell you to start your business by being your own hostess. Some will take it one step further by encouraging you to be your own host whenever there are new products to launch. I am going to tell you to be your own hostess at least once a month. That's right, at least once a month. With today's busy schedules, you will develop a connection to customers who do not have time to be one of your hosts but love shopping in a party environment. Keep an ongoing list of these customers to have an instant guest list. Over time, season after season, the list will grow making it easy for you to find 6 to 10 shoppers who would love to shop at your home. Imagine what this would do for your business if you held just one every month: that would be 12 extra parties a year, increasing your sales on average by $6000 (based on a $500 party). Encourage each guest to bring a friend or two and watch your bookings soar.

There are other fabulous benefits to being your own hostess. In most companies you will be able to access the hostess benefits along with your consultant commissions. Next to purchasing a sample kit, using the hostess benefits program is the best way to affordably add samples to your inventory. I call this **"double dipping"** because you are being paid commission as a consultant and receiving deeply discounted product as a host.

Postcards

One of the tools I used to help me expand my customer base was to carry a postcard sized invitation with me for my next open house, mystery hostess or launch party. I found these to be more effective than business cards. If your company doesn't have a postcard invitation for you to use, create one. This tip makes it easy to be your own host once a month. Carry your invitation with you, when you meet someone new and a conversation about your business ensues, you can hand them an invite. Remember to get their name and number so you can call to give them directions to your home.

Another great way to use postcards is on community and public bulletin boards. I have found them to be more effective than business card because they are eye catching and offer room for you to put a personal note on the back. Using large Avery mailing labels I would print and stick the following message on my postcards:

To place an order,
Book a party,
Or join my team,
Contact Lisa at <insert phone number and email>

Keep It Fresh!

One of the greatest lessons I learned over the years was the importance of having new customers at every party that I did. When your company is brand new or you are new to your company, it is easier to get bookings. Over time, we build a very loyal customer base that we can go back to over and over again, replenishing their favorite products and introducing new additions. My hosts would rebook from season to season, so it was easy to see the same 6 to 10 shoppers every new catalogue. My datebook would be stable and my party average increased. If we are not a conscientious business owner, we can fall into a dangerous trap of just servicing customers and not meeting new ones. This will eventually affect your bookings. To ensure my customer base was always growing and more, importantly, to ensure my host got her full benefits, I coached her to have least two new guests attend with the regulars. Nine out of ten times the new people booked parties.

Bookings Before Sales!

In our fast-paced instant society, we have become conditioned to go straight for the sale, and have forgotten to offer the party. We have become order takers rather than partiers.

In Direct Sales the three step success formula is to book parties, then sell, then recruit. When we put the sale before the booking, we cut ourselves off to that customer's network of friends, family and co-workers, our second and third levels of influence, forcing ourselves to always be searching for the next sale. We work much harder, getting stressed and tired from always prospecting. When we put the focus on the booking first, then provide exceptional hostess coaching, the sales will automatically happen at the party.

Overbook

If you have heard it once, I'm sure you have heard it a thousand times, overbooking is the the golden rule. Learning to be flexible comes with the territory. We are in the people business and cannot predict when illness or emergency will occur. It is a good habit to overbook by twenty five percent. As an example, if you want to hold eight parties a month, you will need to book ten. The practice of overbooking helps you to develop a relaxed, be of service attitude.

PART 2

ASKING FOR THE BOOKING

I would love to get your opinion!

Prior to the successes I achieved at Weekenders, I had unsuccessfully been a sales representative with three other companies that spanned over a 10 year period. I tried my hand at selling cosmetics, home décor and wellness products. So, when I joined Weekenders and was presented with the new consultant quick start challenge, to hold five parties in my first two weeks, I didn't know where to begin. Would my friends and family support me one more time? Fortunately my job as a personal trainer and fitness instructor put me into a very large circle of acquaintances that were the right target market for my product. I decided to skip my first level of influence and jump right into my second. After all, they were women and they wore clothes! Believe it or not, I was extremely shy when I was not leading a fitness class. How would I ever approach these women to help me out? After carefully creating a list of ladies to approach to be my first customers, I decided I would call each of them to invite them to my first party to get their opinion. The calls started with a sincere compliment, followed by, I would love to get your opinion on these fabulous clothes. Each and every one of them was flattered and agreed to attend my new business launch party. After all, what woman doesn't love to give her opinion? The women who attended my first party, just to give me their honest opinion, fell in love with the product and became my first hosts. This technique work so well that I taught it to everyone who joined my team. This phrase works great for fashion companies, home décor, skin care, wellness and food products. No matter what you are selling, it will work for you to start your business and with the introduction of every new product or catalogue.

I would love to get your opinion...
... on our new gourmet spice collection
...on our new Christmas décor
...on our new anti-aging cream
...on our newest designer fragrances
...on our new earring club collection

Can You Help Me?

The only thing a woman likes to do more then give her opinion is to help a friend out. I developed this booking phrase as a nice way to ask for others assistance. After explaining I was working toward a trip or expanding my business, I would ask, "Can you help me out by introducing me to 3-5 ladies that I don't know?" This booking technique worked every time I used it. Asking for an introduction to just a couple friends makes it feel comfortable and easy. I would never get the same positive response if had I asked to be introduced to ten friends. Now that sounds like work. In this context, the word introduce really means party, but because we have asked for help they just can't say no.

This technique became my favorite launch party phrase when I was assisting a new recruit with their first party. I would ask *"Can you help Mary get her business started by introducing her to three to five ladies she doesn't know?"*

This technique is also a great way to ask for referrals.

The "Tentative" Booking

Booking parties tentatively is a basic skill which works cohesively with almost all booking methods. This casual approach should not be taken lightly as 99% of all parties booked tentatively become secure dates.

Here are a couple scripts to try:

If your hostess is unsure of when to book:

"Mary, why don't we book a tentative date and you can get back to me to change your date if it's not convenient for you and your guests?"

If your hostess wants to check with friends before choosing a party date:

"Great! What do you think their first question will be when you tell them you are having a party? That's right, they will ask when? I have a great idea why don't we select two tentative dates for them to choose from. Then you can let me know which one works best for everyone"

If you host is hesitant to give you a date:

"You know Kara by selecting a tentative party date today, Nicole will receive <insert host booking bonus>, but in order to qualify her I need to register your party on my calendar. Now if the date we select turns out not to be good, no problem, we can change it later."

If your goal is to block your calendar, add the following script to your group close, mentioning your upcoming party availability:

"I have a few openings for the end of this month and I am now booking next month." (Remember to block or keep to a three week time frame.)

One mistake direct sellers often make when they are talking about their calendar is to appear to be too available. They do this by saying things like "I can do your party anytime" or "I'm booking parties for this season and next season". One thing I noticed was that whatever I indicated was what they booked. Don't be afraid to book on short notice. Some of the best parties are booked only a few days in advance.

Either/Or

This technique gives the direct seller control over their schedule by always offering the choice of their next two available dates. The prospect host is offered choices so she feels comfortable while the consultant is guiding the bookings to dates she is available.

Here are some scripts to try:

"Mary, I have either Tuesday or Thursday available of next week, which would work better for you?"

"Would you prefer a week day or weekend?"

"Do you like to hold your parties on a Monday or Wednesday evening or a Tuesday or Thursday evening?"

"Would you prefer to have an afternoon or evening party?"

If you were to have a party?

The hypothetical booking is a fun way to confirm a party date. It is kind of like playing pretend with your prospective host. This technique works hand in hand with the available party list compiled from your action calendar. Ask *"If you were to have a party...what day of the week would you want to do it on?"* The response to this question can lead you right into the either/or booking method. This is also a great booking technique to use outside of a party setting when we find ourselves in a conversation with a prospect at the grocery store, doctor's office or at the soccer game.

Do you have your calendar handy?

I discovered this booking technique by accident while making calls one evening. I had a list of women who promised to have a party with me but for one reason or another we didn't have a date yet. Fresh from conference with a new catalogue on my desk to inspire me, I decided to hold a booking blitz and contact these potential hosts. It was easy to make these calls because they had already told me they wanted a party. After enthusiastically teasing them about our new catalogue additions, I told them I had several calls to make but wanted to give them first choice of my available dates. Then I asked, "Do you have your calendar handy?" To my surprise every time I asked, they would get their calendar. Using the either/or booking method would help them select the perfect party date.

Is there any reason why...?

I first read about the Reverse Psychology method in the book "Direct Sales, Be Better Than Good – Be Great" by Joyce M. Ross. Although I understood we have all been programmed as children to say 'no' I didn't really see how this was going to help me book parties. That was until I tried it. Every time I used this phrase, I would get the programmed No response, which in this case means yes.

Here are some of scripts to try:

"Julie is there any reason why we couldn't get a few of your friends together for coffee next week?"

"Brittney is there any reason why I couldn't come to your house to treat you to some free <insert product>?"

"Kaylie is there any reason why you wouldn't want to get that <insert product> off your wish list for free by hosting your own party?"

PART 3

BOOKING AT YOUR PARTIES

Build Desire

Booking bids are quick one-liners that pique interest when thrown out during a presentation. Also known as talks, chatter, dialogue, scripts or invitations, they are one of the most basic and important booking techniques used during a party demonstration. Most companies encourage including three to five bids that create desire to book a party. I am going to challenge that training by encouraging you to slip them in wherever / whenever possible. Attending my first leadership conference the VP of Sales asked me if I would do the training presentation. At the time, I was booking more parties than anyone else in the company and she wanted to figure out why. It became obvious when she lost count at 28 booking talks!

Wouldn't you like it if your clients asked you for a booking? If you can plant enough seeds to create desire, that is exactly what will happen. If you learn to use booking bids effectively, they'll be asking you! The key is to find the words you are comfortable and confidant using. This ensures the conversation feels authentic with a natural non pressure flow. Keep it subtle and relaxed to ensure you are not coming off as an aggressive broken record.

I have found that taking guests on a catalogue tour is a simple and easy presentation style that even the newest recruit can emulate. My thought is, Direct Sales companies invest lots of time and money into creating the perfect business tools, so why not use them. Most catalogues are broken into several different sections outlining the different collections and services. Pick one or two of your favorite items from each section to share with the guests. For most companies that will be between eight and twelve products. It isn't necessary to show every item in the catalogue, as a matter of fact, that can be counterproductive. I've found that most direct sellers get excited when they talk about the products they love the most or the items that are the most popular. To build desire to be a hostess I would include the most expensive from each collection in this line up.

A fun trick is to use Post-it notes because they are the perfect cheat sheet. Create a booking talk to go with each item you plan to share then place the post it note on the page next to it. You don't have to have a photographic memory to purge all of these little scripts. Work them casually into the conversation / demonstration as you feature your favorites.

Try these booking bids on for size:

"I'd love to come to your home and do a party for your family and friends."

"I'm certain by the time I am done our catalogue tour you will be thinking of other ladies who would love our ‹insert product type – jewelry, spices, home decor›"

"Thank you for that suggestion, you know ladies I do requests however a repeat performance is at your house!"

"Our ‹_____› is one of our most popular hostess half price items."

"The ‹_____› is our largest investment piece we carry. More hosts take it for free than any other item."

"Half price is nice and 70% is better but nothing beats FREE!"

"The most affordable way to put this must have item in your ‹closet, cupboard, pantry, home› is to be one of my hosts!"

Create your most popular item!

"More of my hosts purchase this <_____> half price than any other item in our catalogue."

Client File Card / Draw Slip

The client file card is a multi-purpose tool but most of all, it is a reminder to do your booking and recruiting bids. This might be the easiest technique for new business owners to use. Most Direct Sales companies provide Client Card to use but if not you can create your own.

CLIENT CARD	Hostess:		Date:	
Name:			Phone:	
Address:			Cell:	
City:	Postal Code:		Email:	
❑ Yes I would like to receive your monthly Newsletter ❑ Please send me a **Facebook** friend request				
Update me regarding **NEW Products, Sales** and **Fun Events!**	YES	**Maybe** I have a few questions		NO
I would like to receive a **Free Shopping Spree** by hosting a party with my friends.	YES	**Maybe** I have a few questions		NO
I would like more information about becoming a **CONSULTANT**, at no obligation.	YES	**Maybe** I have a few questions		NO

In your demonstration opening script, instruct the guests to complete ONLY the personal information at the top of the form. Name, address, phone numbers, email etc...

At the end of your party, in your demonstration closing, review the questions READ THEM ALOUD reviewing the yes, maybe and no options. Invite them to circle yes, remembering to nod and smile!! Nodding and smiling helps to reinforce a "yes" response.

Collect up the client cards/draw slips to make an inexpensive draw. My favorite thing to give away is a $10 gift certificate that's non transferrable and only redeemable against a party order that night.

After the draw is made, discreetly review the slips using the information gathered to effectively work the room while the guests are shopping.

A YES Response
Book her! Simply say *"So Kelly, when are you thinking of having your party?"* A yes is a yes so don't ask her again. Have a positive expectation and just ask for the date.

A MAYBE Response
Assume she wants to book but has a question. Simply respond with *"So what questions do you have before we book your party?"* Answer her question, overcome any concerns and book a date.

A NO Response

Now there are two kinds of No's. The no you can turn into a yes and the no that really means no. Don't let the no response intimidate you into doing nothing. If the guest was very interactive, had lots of fun and you are surprised by her answer then you might be able to turn her around. I have turned many of these no's into a yes by jokingly saying *"Sherri I can't believe you aren't booking a party!!"* Wait for her response and overcome the concern/objection. Or be a bit softer by saying *"Cheryl I notice that you said no on your draw slip to having your own party, can I ask why?"* Wait for her response, overcome the concern and encourage her to select a party date.

If you can only implement one idea from this book make it the Client File Card / Draw Slip. For 20 years I have used this technique successfully and taught it to hundreds of direct sellers to increase their booking odds. From time to time over my career, I've abandoned this practice to make way for new ideas, and suffered disastrous results.

There is another very important reason I want to encourage you to use this manual customer tracking method. On June 9, 2008 I woke up ready to greet my business day as usual, only to discover the company

I loved was gone. They had declared bankruptcy over the weekend locking consultants out of the back office. Fortunately I had been using the client file cards and had taught my downline to do the same. Picking up the pieces was easier for us than for most. This might be the worst case scenario but there are many reasons why you might not be able to access the company back office. Computers crash, power failures, systems change, we can leave or even be asked to leave. A smart business owner protects their information.

Booking Envelopes

This technique might just be the softest but most effective bid of them all. No matter what your direct sales experience is, you will find it is a comfortable way to make your next party dates available. Take three hostess planning packages (or booking envelopes), on the top right hand corner; mark your next 3 available dates. Put only one date on each corner of the envelope. Fan the envelopes out on the table so the dates can easily be seen by the guests. Now include the following script in your demonstration:

"Ladies, for your convenience I have marked my next three available dates on the hostess planning packages that are on the table (point to them). To book your party, simply select the date which works best for you and bring me the package when you are ready to place your order. If these dates don't work, please let me know and we can find a date that will work for you and your friends."

Available Party List

Creating a list of your available dates to pass around at your parties is an easy cheat sheet. On a piece of paper list only your next three or four party available dates, placed it on the coffee or display table, draw reference to it during your party closing then pass it around.

Here is a sample booking bids to use with your available party list:

"If you have fallen in love with 3 or 4 items then you should take advantage of our Hostess Benefits and have me treat you to some Free and half price of items. For your convenience I will pass around a list of my available party dates. To book your party mark your name beside the date you want. If these dates don't work let me know and we can find one that will work for you and your friends."

This technique can also be modified to be used in a newsletter, tweet or face book message. My good friend Denise is a spicy gal that has built a successful home based business. She is passionate about her monthly customer newsletter. The company she represents offers a professional one for consultants to use but she chooses to draft her own. Each month she writes a personal message, adds in product tips, the company monthly customer, hostess, and business opportunity specials. Below the hostess offers she will list her available party dates. This monthly practice generates, depending on the time of year, two or more group parties plus a couple requests for catalogue parties.   That is over two dozen additional parties a year! Denise feels the secret to her success is consistency and relationship building.

Here is a sample of how Denise lists her available party dates:

My available dates for November Parties:

November 2, 7 afternoon, 9, 12, 14 afternoon, 16, 18, 19, 21 afternoon and 30th

Book and Hold Gifts

Many consultants like to offer a booking gift as an extra bonus incentive for holding a party. I am a big fan of offering extra incentives when you need to fill your calendar and the company may not be running any additional hostess promotions. One mistake consultants often make is to give the gift upon dating the party. Once the gift is in the host's hand there is no extra incentive for them to hold their commitment. My personal practice was to make it a book and hold gift. I would happily present them with the gift the night they hold their party.

A few examples of what I might offer are:
1. 50% off any item of their choice
2. A free accessory
3. No taxes or shipping
4. A gift basket of product

Viola is a passionate business woman. She is a successful leader who is very social media savvy. Her creative posts get lots of attention from her face book friends. Wanting to book a few extra parties Viola posted this message:

"Text text and more texts CONTEST! BOOK YOUR PARTY via text, choose your date and time and text me @ ###-###-####, you will automatically receive the $50 basket of favorites just for texting and holding a party! (Catalog parties included) CONTEST is TODAY ONLY!!! Booking parties in ALL of North America!!! TEXT NOW!!!"

Viola's offer is the perfect example of a book and hold incentive and proof that the basic booking techniques work when applied to social media situations. Viola booked 6 new parties from this one face book posting!

Stack the Hostess Benefits

Did you know that 65% of the population are visual learners and that 90% of the information that the brain receives is visual? It is for these reasons that stacking the benefits is one of the strongest booking techniques that can be used. When combined with great booking bids results are guaranteed.

Stacking the benefits creates a visual of what she will earn based on your company hostess reward program. Using this page of the catalogue and your product kit create a breakdown of the savings. Use the company party average as the inspiration to create the display. This ensures the audience keeps an open mind as everyone can visualize themselves hosting an average party.

Most companies offer free and discounted merchandise. To create the biggest visual possible, take the most expensive items at the discounted rate, than use the most popular items to show how they can be earned for free.

Rebook Your Hostess

Rebooking a hostess is vital to building a loyal customer base. Approximately ninety percent of my hosts rebooked me for the same or following season. This was due to the positive working relationship I developed with my hosts but also because I assumed they wanted to see me again. With my calendar in hand, ready to book a tentative date, I would say, "*So Sally, when would you like to hold your <fall or spring> party? I'm sure that everyone here is going to want to see the new catalgoue.*"

It is our job as consultants to ensure she gets the maximum benefits possible at her party. Often rebooking is the answer.

The practice of rebooking your five stars hosts into the next season will ensure your date book is full and you are ready to party when the new products are launched. There is no greater reassurance than walking into a new season with ten or more parties lined up.

Objections

Be prepared to overcome the common booking objections. Consider objections a normal part of business. I always look at them as problems that require solutions and you are the solution maker. The prospect is depending on you to solve her problem.

My approach to objections is different from most direct sales experts. Instead of telling you to use the very dated "feel, felt, found" technique I am going to encourage you to keep a diary. Yup, journal about the objections you receive. Objections are just problems that need solutions and you are the solution maker! Every direct seller will encourage different objections. These objections will be based on their target market and party plan experience. You will notice more experienced and successful direct sellers encounter fewer objections. The reason for this is that they have perfected their scripts and demonstrations overcoming objections before they even get them. That really is the secret. So it is my recommendation that you track your objection patterns by keeping a booking objections diary. List the objections you receive and write out two solutions for each one:

Solution #1 will be a presentation script that provides a solution during the demonstration. This will help to eliminate the objection before the private close.

Solution #2 is your response to overcome the objection during the private close.

Here is an example for the common objection
"I'm too busy"

Presentation Script: *" Busy women love to shop with <_____> because it is a great way to save time, offers an opportunity to socialize with friends or family and when you book your own presentation you'll be saving money too!*

Group Close: *"DO you know ladies, that planning a party takes no more time than it did coming here tonight. All you need to do is invite a few friends, put on the coffee and I'll do the rest!"*

"Always be prepared to overcome objections. Objections are nothing more than problems that need a solution and you are the solution maker!"

The Perfect Uniform

Since "The Woman's Dress for Success" guide was written in 1977 things have changed. Yet, picking the perfect business uniform can make a big difference in your booking and sales success. I'm not going to go into a big debate of whether you should wear a business suit or dress more casual at your parties. That conversation might be more about your personal style and company image. My goal is to educate you a little bit about colour. The biggest mistake direct sellers make is dressing in black. Although black can be elegant and slimming, it is the most aggressive colour on the color wheel, especially when combined with white. Dressing all in black can make you appear intimidating or aggressive. Now if you want to be taken seriously, then avoid soft pink which is generally the colour reserved for baby girls. Colour might seem like a little thing, but it could make a big difference in how your guests perceive you, especially when sitting at the private closing desk, face to face, asking for the sale and offering the booking.

Part 4

Post Party

Rate Your Hostess

My mentor Anne taught me the value of rating my hosts, now I want to share this system with you. This practice helps a direct seller focus on working smart not hard. In this relationship driven industry, rating your hosts keeps you grounded to producing results. To ensure future business success, reduce postponements, increase bookings and party sales, I recommended rating your parties, using the following five star method:

5 Stars

$1000+ with two or more bookings. Top priority for future dates

4 Stars

$700 - $900 with two or more bookings. Top priority for future dates

3 Stars

Average $500 - $600 with one - two bookings. Top priority for future dates

2 Stars

$300 - $400 with one booking. Provide extra host coaching

1 Star

Low sales, postpones or cancels, no future bookings. Do not rebook

Here is a true success story: Deb was a real go getter with an infectious positive attitude that got others excited. In a coaching session, she shared with me that it was her goal to be in the company top 10 in sales at the next convention. That meant growing her business by $20,000. A pretty lofty goal to sell $100K! To get an overview of her business, we rated the hosts in her calendar. The goal was for every party she held to be a five star experience. She provided additional coaching to her average hosts, helping them increase their party sales, a win/win for both of them. Then she offered her one star hosts the opportunity to hold private shopping appointments or attend one of her open houses, making room in her schedule for more five star hosts. Adding this practice to Deb's business increased her party sales average while eliminating postponements and cancellations. She was recognized on stage at at the next convention with sales in excess of $112K!

Let Go

Learning to let go was very difficult for me as a new direct seller but it was a skill I developed with experience. In the early days, I would hold on to a booking like a dog with a bone, not willing to let them out of their end of the deal, no matter what the circumstances. I'd become the queen of overcoming objections. A title I proudly held onto until it dawned on me that this practice wasn't making me any friends or any money. It might seem strange that I am bringing this up in a booking -- "how to guide", so let me explain. If, on average, I was earning $150 for every party I held, that would mean that I was losing $150 every time that I rebooked the chronic postponer. What you need understand is that you cut your losses by moving on to a new enthusiastic host who really wants to have a party. Introducing the 5 star rating system broke me of this bad business practice.

I recall a consultant on my team who put herself out of business by not letting go. Her name was Irene, a single mom of three, who desperately needed to make some extra cash fast. After holding her launch party it became apparent to me that her circle of influence, friends and family, were not very affluent party goers. Irene wanted to be successful and, instead of looking for new hosts outside her immediate circle, she began going in circles with her friends and family.

They would book a party date and then reschedule, once, twice, then cancel all together. After a very frustrating couple of weeks, Irene called me to say she had given it her all but the business was just not for her.

"When the horse is dead... get off!"
~ Rosita Ayala Perez

CUSTOMER CARE CALLS

Customer care calls can be a great way to find new bookings. Nicole one of the consultants on my team had horrible phone phobia. I encouraged her to set her fears aside and to call the customers that had recently placed orders with her. To pretend she was calling an old friend she hadn't seen in a while. Nicole was a good student who always accepted a challenge. I will never forget her words after spending an evening of making customer care calls. The light bulb went gone off and with new found enthusiasm she exclaimed "I get it, it PAYS to work on the phone!" It sure does. It pays in add -- on orders, new bookings and even recruits. I recommend that you schedule one night a week to make customer care calls.

Here is an example of my script and the seven points to cover on each call:

Customer Care Call Script

"Hello, this is <Insert Your Full Name> calling. (Pause for response) If you recall, I'm your <company name> consultant, we met at <hosts name> Party. (Pause for response) The reason I am calling is to make a quick customer care call. Is this a convenient time to talk? (Pause for response) GREAT!..."

- **Customer Service:**

  "First of all, I'd like thank you for attending ‹insert hosts name› party and want to to be sure that you are enjoying ‹ Refer to items they specifically purchased› that you ordered. Great, we love to keep our customers happy."

- **The Telephone Order**

  "Our current Catalogue will soon be retired. So, as an end of season special I am offering No Taxes on all telephone orders (or insert current company customer offer). *Was there anything that you had on your wish list from this catalogue?"* (Suggest add on items based on previous purchases)

- **Stock Sample Sales**

  "In just a couple of week's time I will be selling my samples at a ‹insert percentage› discount. Would you like to know what samples I have available?"

- **Ask for the Bookings**

  "Our new catalogue is about to arrive and I look forward to sharing it to you. Is there any reason why you couldn't bring a small group of ladies together in your home or mine? It is easy and fun. I have ‹insert date› and ‹insert date› available for a booking."

- Offer the Business Opportunity:

  "You know this time of the season is especially good to join <insert company>! Have you ever thought of doing what I do either part time or casually? I think you would really benefit from buying our products wholesale, the tax benefits and earning extra income. Could we get together for a half an hour over coffee or on the phone and I could let you know more about this incredible opportunity. How does this sound?"

- Extent an Event Invitation:

  "I would like to have you as my special guest at our, <Insert new company special event details>. This evening fun and informative evening is in appreciation of our loyal clients and hostesses."

- Resolve Quality Issues:

  "No problem, I will be happy to return it to the company for testing and we will do our best to satisfy you. Let's get this looked after right away. When can I pick it up, or would you prefer to drop it off to me?"

"Treat every customer as if they sign your paycheck...because they do!"

~Author Unknown

Even the busiest of consultant can offer great customer service. Sheri was a rising superstar on my team. She worked a full time job, had a busy family life and lived on farm. Holding three or four parties a week and building a strong team Sheri's business was on fire. Her days were filled with family activities and farm chores but she never made excuses. Each customer would receive a "thank you" for your order email or text as part of her ordering responsibilities. Sheri believes this is one of the reasons she is so successful and her customer base is so loyal.

Another great way to provide customer service follow up is via your face book fan page. My friend Mary posted these messages on her wall as conversation starters:

"Mary is running a 72 hour SIZZLING SUMMER SALE! Message me ASAP!"

"Mary is getting ready for a HUGE April fashion sale! April 1st call me to book your show or place an order - amazing sales begin April 1st - no fooling!"

"If you don't take care of your customers, someone else will."
~Author Unknown

Customer Rescue

If you are a veteran who has been a direct seller for several seasons; maybe even years, then a client rescue might be just what you need to pump up the parties in your calendar. This is a great exercise because you already have a customer and hostess following. Sometimes we lose track of great people in the process of building our business. It is never too late to go back and scoop them up.

After compiling a list of the customers you wish to rescue, create a "Hi, remember me" rescue letter. This letter should encourage them to contact you by including a gift certificate.

I found that the rescue program worked best when I mailed a new catalogue with the letter and enclosed a $10 gift certificate. To keep it affordable and follow up manageable, I recommend doing only five or ten letters every week or two. **Never send more letters out than you are prepared to follow up with.**

Here is a sample of the letter that I used:

Dear Valued Customer:

I am sending you this letter to say hello and to let you know that I am still a Fashion Consultant with Weekenders.

If at this time you are already affiliated with another Consultant and happy, I wish you continued fashion success. However, if you are not, I would be pleased to serve you and your friends with my fashion expertise.

I am very excited about the new Collection and would love to share it with you. Please find enclosed a catalogue and a $10.00 gift certificate that may be used toward your next private presentation, phone order or group fashion presentation.

I truly value your business and I will be calling you to see when we can get together. **As an added bonus, if you call me before I call you, I will double your gift certificate to $20.00** (with a minimum order of $75.00). I look forward to speaking with you in the very near future.

Fashionably yours,

10 Reasons You Don't Get Bookings

In Direct Sales it is our goal to successfully obtain two or more new bookings from each party we hold. If this does not occur, it maybe for one or more of the following reasons:

1. Weak booking bids or no bookings bids at all.
2. Presentation scripts are not creating desire for the product or to book.
3. Hosting a party appears like a lot of work or appears time consuming.
4. Hostess served too much food.
5. Demonstration portion of the evening is too long.
6. No privacy to write up the orders.
7. Forgot to offer each guest the opportunity to book their own party during the private close or asking incorrectly.
8. Not overcoming objections during the private close.
9. Unprofessional personal image or attitude.
10. Not building a positive rapport with guests.

About The Author

Lisa Toovey is no stranger to the direct sales industry, as a matter of fact, after 30 years she feels she has a Party Plan PhD™. Her direct sales journey began at the age of 16 when her mother signed her up as a recruit for a cousin so she could win a challenge. Lisa had no idea that, that experience would leave her searching for more.

Next came a home décor company and then on to a wellness company, all great learning experiences and training but no real success. What she learned along the way was that to be successful it is necessary to have passion for the product you demonstrate, faith and trust in the company you represent and when you add a dash of enthusiasm, it can be magical. That is how she would describe her next 16 years of success with Weekenders. From 1992 – 2008 Lisa built a multi-million dollar organization with Weekenders, reaching her company's Circle of Excellence for 13 consecutive years, earning numerous sales and leadership Awards. She has been coaching and training since 1993 and has a deep understanding of the challenges and needs of the independent direct sales professional. To better assist her sales group in their goals, Lisa completed the Results Centered Leadership Coaching Program in 1999.

In 2006 Lisa was a "Manitoba Woman Entrepreneur of the Year" Finalist.

Motivated to help others, Lisa co-founded "Directions Unlimited" in 2007, Manitoba's networking group for direct sellers and multi-level marketing professionals. Today over thirty different companies make up the membership and embrace the show, share, and support philosophies.

Lisa created "Directly Speaking with Lisa Toovey" in 2008, and since then has had the pleasure of working as a speaker, coach, trainer and corporate consultant for many direct sales companies. As the author of "Directly Speaking about Bookings", she also wrote the "Epicure Selections" and "Sunset Gourmet" Consultant's Guides. These tools have helped thousands of direct sellers to learn the basics skills of party plan.

Next she assisted in bringing "Jockey Person to Person" to Canada as a pioneering consultant and leader, building another successful organization. Then retired from the field in October of 2010, to become a Canadian Regional Sales Manager, working as a coach and trainer for several direct sales companies.

Lisa continues to train and share with other direct sellers. You can find her at www.directlyspeaking.ca or email her at lisa@directlyspeaking.ca

A special thank you to my friends for their contributions to this book:

Lucille Williams

Laura Barkman

Viola Bauer

Denise Hildebrand

Mary Shifano

The following sources were quoted or used as reference in the making this book. I wish to extend a special acknowledgement to:

Anne Craig – Group VP, Jockey P2P

Belinda Ellsworth – Step into Success

Patrice Matteson – Dynamic Production, Inc

Joyce M Ross – Direct Sales Be Better Than Good Be Great!